Getting Better Slowly

by Nick Wood

An inspiring story of illness and recovery

Published by Playdead Press 2016

© Nick Wood 2016

Nick Wood has asserted his rights under the Copyright, Design and Patents Act, 1988, to be identified as the authors of this work.

A CIP catalogue record for this book is available from the British Library.

ISBN 978-1-910067-42-0

Caution
All rights whatsoever in this play are strictly reserved and application for performance should be sought through the author before rehearsals begin. No performance may be given unless a license has been obtained.

This book is sold subject to the condition that it shall not by way of trade or otherwise, be lent, resold, hired out, or otherwise circulated without the publisher's prior consent in any form of binding or cover other than that in which it is published and without a similar condition including this condition being imposed on the subsequent purchaser.

Playdead Press
www.playdeadpress.com

Getting Better Slowly premiered at the Lincoln Drill Hall on 22nd September 2016 ahead of a national tour.

Performed by **Adam Pownall & Kitty Randle**
Creative Producer – **Adam Pownall**
Director – **Tilly Branson**
Movement Director – **Marc Brew**
Writer – **Nick Wood**
Composer – **Poetical Machines Ltd**
Designer – **Kate Unwin**
Production Manager – **Laura Stone**
Associate Choreographer – **Kimberley Harvey**
Associate Dramaturg – **Luca Rutherford**
Lighting Design – **Howell Thomas**
Assistant Producer – **Martyn Bignell**

Commissioned by GAIN Charity, Arts Council England, Core Lincolnshire One Venues & Lincoln Drill Hall

With support from ARC Stockton, Deda Derby & In Good Company

The script was published before rehearsals were finished, and there may be small differences in performance.

Notes from the Director

In November 2015 we spent two weeks developing some of the early ideas for *Getting Better Slowly*. An audience member who came to the see the early scenes we shared wrote an email to Adam afterwards saying *What insights into the relationship between our minds and bodies can you share with us? You're like a space man. You've been to the moon and we want to know not just what it was like, but what did you 'see'?* I had known Adam for several years before he mentioned anything to me about his 'journey to the moon', but when he did, I was immediately struck by how universally relatable his story was. None of us know what is around the corner, when an illness or accident might affect us or someone we love, and how we might deal with its effects, *how it might change us*. It's been a great adventure working out how best to tell Adam's story, how to share the physical and emotional journey he has been on, and working with such a talented and diverse team of creatives to do that. I hope that the resulting performance is a positive and inspiring experience, and raises awareness of GBS and of the realities of dealing with any situation where we realise we are not always in total control of our own bodies and health.

Tilly Branson

Notes from the Author

You might think that researching and writing a story that charts the progress of a serious illness involving total paralysis followed by slow and uncertain recovery would be a pretty serious business, and of course, it was. But it was also a hugely enjoyable one, and if that sounds weird, even disrespectful, then you haven't met Adam and his family. They went through this awful experience with grace and the stubborn determination to be positive, no matter what the outcome, but, because that's who they are, they also found humour in even the darkest moments.

For some reason Adam, on what was, let's face it, a pretty slight acquaintance, decided to trust me with his story, and because of Adam's faith in me his family trusted me too, sight unseen. As he took me through the stages of his illness and recovery, he held nothing back, he took me into the worst moments. Sometimes on the tapes we made there are gaps, silence, moments when the memories got too much, when he'd take a breath, collect himself and carry on. Although I often wanted to, he never asked to stop, never dodged a question. But there's laughter on those tapes too, as he recounts the many indignities that accompany serious illness, remembers the moments of black humour. Talking to all the family I got used to hearing variants of the phrase 'It wasn't funny at the time but....'.

Being trusted by his family was both intimidating and moving. At least I got to know Adam before we embarked on the taping sessions. His family allowed to me walk into homes I'd never visited and ask people I'd never met to relive one of the worst experience of their lives, on tape, in front of a stranger. I was terrified of letting them down. How they did it with such generosity and honesty I have no idea, but they did, and without their contribution there would have been no play.

None of us on the creative team want to make Adam and his family out to be heroes, they wouldn't allow it. As one of them said, 'When stuff like this happens you just get on with it, don't you?'. Adam didn't survive and recover because he 'fought hard'. That carries the lazy journalistic implication that those who don't survive are at least partly to blame because they obviously haven't 'fought hard' enough. The family's collective courage and determination certainly helped him cope, but his recovery and the extent of that recovery, as it always is, was down to a combination of medical skill and luck. However, and I haven't asked the others, I think if anything serious was ever to happen to any of us, they've put down a marker on the way we should try to behave.

Nick Wood

Cast and Creative

Adam Pownall | Creative Producer/Performer
Adam is a Theatre Programmer and Producer in the UK, and currently Artistic Manager of the Lincoln Drill Hall following programming for Derby Theatre. In 2014 he won the Olwen Wymark Award for supporting New Writing within Theatre for the Writer's Guild for his work in opening and running Create Theatre, a state of the art studio theatre in Mansfield. He specialises in supporting emerging companies, artist development and new-writing and is a proud advocate for regional theatre in the East Midlands.
@adam_pablo

Kitty Randle | Performer
Kitty's theatre credits include: Flee in *The Unfurling of Indigo Higgins* (Arletty Theatre), Chief in Babbling Vagabonds' *Naughty Meg* (Derby Live), Vanessa Bell in Moving Stories' *Vanessa and Virginia* (Riverside Studios and international tour), Mrs. Usher / Annie Besant in *Sweet Comradeship*, Electra in *Orestes: Re-Examined* (Southwark Playhouse), Violet in *Heresies* (Bristol Old Vic Studio) and Susanna Walcott in *The Crucible* (Sheffield Theatres). TV: *4 O'Clock Club*, *Emmerdale*. Film: Sarah in *Blackout*. Kitty is also co-founder and core artist of Moving Stories Theatre Company.
@kittyrandle

Director | Tilly Branson
Tilly Branson's past work includes *Acting Alone* (International tour 2015-16), *Man to Man* (Mercury Theatre Colchester 2013 and Park Theatre London 2014), *Entertaining Angels*, *Due Course* and *Goldfish* (New Perspectives, rural tours 2012-2014) and *End to End* (The Gramophones, Edinburgh Fringe/touring). For the past four years she has been working on an AHRC funded practice-based PhD about rural touring. tillybranson.com @tillybranson

Movement Director | Marc Brew
Marc has been working as a dancer, choreographer and director for more than 20 years in the UK and abroad. In 2014 Marc was nominated for Outstanding Achievement in Performance (Individual) at the prestigious Isadora Duncan Awards for his solo piece *Remember When*. In 2015, his autobiographical piece *For Now, I am...* explored what it is to be broken and reborn, the first work he has made that engages directly with his body since a head-on car crash in 1997 left him with a spinal cord injury. He is currently Guest Artistic Director at AXIS Dance Company and Associate Artistic Director at Ballet Cymru.
@marc_brew

Writer | Nick Wood
Nick's commissions include scripts for Radio 4, Derby Theatre, Thalia Theatre Hamburg, Action Transport, Theatr Iolo, Hans Otto Potsdam, RSC, and Eastern Angles. He recently returned to acting, touring his own

play *A Girl With A Book*. He's proud to be associated with Adam's project and feels very lucky as his adaptation of *The Underground Man* opens at Nottingham Playhouse on the same night as *Getting Better Slowly*.
@nickwood39

Composer | Poetical Machines Ltd
Poetical Machines Ltd. create bespoke music and audio fx for live theatre, dance productions, film, radio, museums and galleries in addition to developing drama projects based on science and technology themes and producing podcasts and web content from their studio in Derby.
poeticalmachines.co.uk
@PoeticalMachine

Designer | Kate Unwin
Kate has worked as a freelance set and costume designer for the past fifteen years. Working predominately in theatre, Kate has worked for the National Theatre, London's West End, regional theatres all over the UK and designed many touring and outdoor productions for Europe and the Middle East. She also designs site specific work, installations, bespoke costumes, events, music videos and has had a Best Set Design nomination from the Off West End
Awards. www.kateunwin.co.uk @kateunwindesign

Production Manager | Laura Stone
Laura is a stage manager based in Birmingham. She trained in Theatre Design at Nottingham Trent University

and also works as a designer. Her stage management credits include BE Festival at Birmingham REP Theatre and the recent debut tour of *Top Table* by Richard Stone. @lestonedesign

Associate Choreographer | Kimberley Harvey
Kimberley Harvey is a freelance performer, choreographer and dance teacher.
Alongside this, she's a Candoco Artist, which includes teaching for Candoco Dance Company nationally and internationally. Kimberley has her own company, Subtle Kraft Co. Their work stems from what it means to be human and the creative potential of relationships.
www.subtlekraft.co @Kimblecake

Associate Dramaturg | Luca Rutherford
Luca is a writer and performer based in Newcastle and an Associate Artist of ARC Stockton.
She believes in making art accessible and theatre that is non-exclusive in form and content. Luca has nationally toured her solo show *Learning How To Die*, directed by Iain Bloomfield and with script advice from Chris Thorpe. She is currently working with Alex Swift and Seiriol Davies on a new children's show; with Unlimited Theatre as an engagement practitioner; and performing with Action Transport Theatre and Unity Theatre's production of *Little Red and The Big Bad Wolf*.
@LucaRutherford

Lighting Design | Howell Thomas

Lighting Designer Howell Thomas's recent work credits *A Beautiful Thing* (UK tour 2015), White light and Sakura installation (Doddington Hall 2015) and *Phantom of the Opera* (Lincoln Drill Hall 2016). Theatre design projects include UK tours of *Bouncers*, *50 days of Grey* (2013), *Art* (2012), *Misery* (2011), the Pasadena Roof Orchestra (2011) and working credits including LTR, ROH, Channel 4, BBC Symphony Orchestra ,The Hallé, Swansea Grand, NYT, NYTW, National Literature Centre of Wales, CIA. He currently holds a lecturing post in Lincoln and is resident Lighting Designer at Doddington Hall and JMP Productions.

Acknowledgements

We would like to thank the following individuals for their exceptional contributions to and ongoing support of *Getting Better Slowly*:

The NHS; Our Crowdfunders; GAIN Charity; Caroline Morrice; Lincoln Drill Hall; ARC Stockton; Annabel Turpin; Deda Derby; Stephen Munn; Derby Theatre; Sarah Brigham; Ruby Glaskin; In Good Company; Rob Day; Swainson Productions; Lincolnshire One Venues; The Scenery Shop; Chris Kirkwood; Gavin Street; Andrew McIntyre; Toby Ealden; Zest Theatre; Simon Johnson; Emma Pownall; Macauley Dixon; Dr John Winer; Lincoln Performing Arts Centre; Nathan Haines; Lincoln Hospital Trust; Sam Grogan; Laura Lindsay; Trina Haldar; Debbie McAndrew. It goes without saying we'd like to express our gratitude to our families and friends who have supported us on this artistic journey.

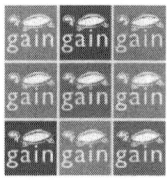

Guillain-Barré & Associated Inflammatory Neuropathies (GAIN) exists to:

• Support patients and families through a range of services which will help them understand and manage their conditions;
• Promote and facilitate both clinical and non-clinical research to improve the lives of those affected by these conditions; and
• Promote understanding of these conditions among the public and medical and social healthcare professionals.

Guillain-Barré syndrome is an acute condition affecting the peripheral nerves, in which the body's immune system attacks the myelin sheath (insulating coating of the nerves). This leads to the short-circuiting of the nerve signals which causes sudden weakness resulting in paralysis and a loss of sensation, often but not always with severe pain. The worst degree of weakness is usually reached within 4 weeks and always within 6 weeks. Recovery can take a few weeks or many months.

Some patients develop a similar but longer-lasting condition called CIDP (chronic inflammatory demyelinating polyradiculoneuropathy). CIDP, once known as 'chronic GBS', is now usually regarded as a related condition, as are a number of other variants, both acute and chronic. It is possible to recover from CIDP, but many will be affected for the rest of their lives and will require ongoing treatment. GBS/CIDP is neither hereditary nor contagious, nor is it age or gender-related.

Around 1,200 people are affected by GBS annually in the UK with a further 500 being diagnosed with CIDP. About 80% of those with GBS will make a good recovery, but unfortunately between 5-10% of people will die as a result of the condition and the other 10-15% may experience long term residual effects ranging from limited mobility or dexterity, to life-long dependency on a wheelchair.

GAIN receives no government funding, relying on the generosity of the public to support our work. Further information about our work can be found at

www.gaincharity.org.uk
or contact *director@gaincharity.org.uk*

GETTING BETTER SLOWLY.

As the audience arrive Adam and Kitty are there talking to them. The house lights come down.

INTRODUCTION

ADAM: It's hard to know where to start, to tell you how it all began for me, I don't mean 'how it all began' *(gestures to indicate birth)* but how it started, the illness, the GBS,

KITTY: The Gary Barry Syndrome.

ADAM: The Guillain-Barré Syndrome. It started on a Saturday night.

KITTY: Hold on a minute.

ADAM: What?

KITTY: If we're going to tell the story of your illness we need to know what kind of a person you were before it started.

ADAM: Do we?

KITTY: We do.

Kitty moves Adam through a whistle-stop of his life before GBS. Before she can do so Adam stops her and shows us one aspect of what he was like, smoothing his hair, straightening his clothes. He grins at her, he's ready.

AUDIO
A collage of voices/sounds –
Adam – talking about his work etc – and possibly just onwards from there talking about him working in Derby and the bar.

Adam's mum – (Perhaps Adam could acknowledge that it's his mum's voice as he's moved at pace by Kitty – 'My mum!') "I'll say this for Adam right, he worked hard and played hard…' – ' Do you know what - When he was took ill he had thirteen jobs…'

KITTY: Youth Theatre, workshops, dance class…

ADAM: Yeah, dance class…

KITTY: Stand straight. Feet directly below your hips, shoulders relaxed… Arms out to the sides… And raise them above your head… and hang. *(moves into the physio exercises with a touch of GBS character)* And push with your legs. Push with your arms. What day is it? How old are you? Can you name the Prime Minister…

ADAM: No, that's not right...

KITTY: No, it isn't is it? Sorry, mustn't get ahead of ourselves, must we? *(back to what he did before the illness)* Tangere Arts. Clubbing. Standing on the touchline supporting your nephew and thinking...

ADAM: ...One of these days I must get round to joining a team and start playing properly.

KITTY: Working on the bar at Saints to help out the manager...

ADAM: My cousin Katie. I was working the night it started.

KITTY: A Saturday night.

ADAM: March 2009.

KITTY: Closing time at Saints. I'm going to play Katie.

ADAM: And I'm going to play...

KITTY: Adam?

SATURDAY NIGHT.

KITTY: Close down the bar.

ADAM: Turn off the lights.

KITTY: Lock the doors and ...

BOTH: Hit the clubs!

Movement section ends.

Adam and Katy, not drunk, but certainly not sober.

ADAM: Taxi?

KATY: Home?

ADAM: Your place?

KATY: My place.

ADAM: Great night.

KATY: Great night.

BOTH: Bed.

They collapse on to separate beds.

GBS APPEARS.

Kitty moves into the character of GBS

ADAM: Who are you?

KITTY: You invited me in.

ADAM: That isn't what I asked. And no, I didn't.

KITTY: Invited might be stretching a point. Let's say your body made it possible for us to be together.

ADAM: What are you doing here? Look, in case you haven't realised, I'm not interested...

KITTY: I've come to help.

ADAM: I don't need help. Tell me who you are.

KITTY: I can't.

ADAM: Tell me who you are.

Movement section.

KITTY: Where you're heading they're going to love me.

ADAM: I'm not going anywhere.

KITTY: Neither am I. Accept it – it's fate – you and I are destined to become intimately acquainted.

ADAM FALLING ILL.

Adam still. Unwell, puzzled. Kitty takes him deeper into the illness leading him through the first symptoms. Adam remembering and experiencing at the same moment.

KITTY: You feel like you've got ...

ADAM: ...a bad hangover that won't go away.

KITTY: When you all sit down for lunch on the Sunday...

ADAM: ...Mother's Day.

KITTY: You've got pins and needles in your hands and feet.

ADAM: I went to work on the Monday.

KITTY: But on Tuesday you pulled a sickie because...

ADAM: I'm wiped out, sorry, it must be a bug...

KITTY: You've got no energy, your leg's hurting,

ADAM: The pain's moved into my shoulder.

KITTY: You can't get out of bed. This isn't man 'flu – You're really sick.

AUDIO – Adam's Mum – 'I can remember saying, like, he's not even bothered about his phone, so he's ill, I know he's really ill, because you know what they're like with their phones.'

Adam moves out of the moment to reflect on what happened to him.

ADAM: Physically, for me, it began in my feet. When I woke up they felt cold. Like they'd been stuck out the end of the duvet all night. But they didn't warm up. Then they started to tingle. As if I'd been dancing all night in too tight shoes. As for the rest of me, yes, it could have been a hangover, but hangovers wear off.

Look. You're sitting down. Like I was that morning. Just try and concentrate on your feet for a moment. Feel them inside your shoes. Where they touch the shoes, on the sides, the toe, the heel, the sole. There's something not quite as it should be. Are they cold? If they are, are they colder than they should be? Is it you imagining they don't feel right, or do they really not feel right? Is something wrong? And is that feeling of 'not rightness' starting to move up your legs?

Kitty enters the moment as the performer.

KITTY: Any hypochondriacs in tonight? When you don't feel well what do you do?

ADAM: You go to the doctor.

KITTY: Three times in almost as many days.

ADAM: Visit One.

Adam moves a chair inviting Kitty to sit on it. He takes the role of the doctor. He prevents Kitty from speaking even though she tries to.

ADAM: What's the problem? You don't feel right. You've got cold feet. All the time. They tingle, they ache...

It sounds like flu. You've got flu.

Take some paracetamol, lots of fluids, and have a few days in bed.

KITTY: Visit Two.

ADAM: No better? No change? Ah, you feel pain rather than numbness and it's 'sort of moved into your shoulder'. You've probably trapped a nerve.

KITTY: It's not just my feet anymore, My legs are hurting.

ADAM: I think perhaps I should give you a rectal exam.

KITTY: What? Why?

ADAM: We have to eliminate all the possibilities.

KITTY: Which are?

ADAM: Everything and anything.

KITTY: I'm not at all sure about this…

ADAM: We can't reach a diagnosis without all the facts.

A piece of movement that isn't entirely comical but does show the invasiveness and indignity involved. (Possibly with them enacting the moment briefly apart from each other?)

KITTY: So what did that tell you?

ADAM: Absolutely nothing. Look, you feel ill, you've got no energy, in my opinion, it's probably a virus. Painkillers. Bed. Rest.

Kitty takes on the role of Emma.

KITTY: Visit Three.

ADAM: Good morning. No better, I see.

Pause.

KITTY: It was a different doctor.

ADAM: Good morning. No better, I see.

EMMA: This is the third time Adam's been here this week. I've had to bring him this time because he can't even get out of the house on his own. I'm his sister. He's getting worse. He was sick all last night. He's losing the feeling in his arms and his legs and now he's saying it's his chest. And it's not flu.

// indicates where Emma stops the doctor's attempts to speak.

// Your colleague's already given him a rectal exam, I can't see any point in giving him another. // He's had painkillers and they don't make any difference. Fine. Good. Give him a blood test. // We can't wait for the results until Monday. We need them now. Leave it, just leave it. It'll be quicker for me to drive him to the hospital and take the bloods myself. // Yes, I do know what I'm talking about. I'm a nurse.

AUDIO – Emma – 'I took him up to King's Mill, couldn't get him out of the car, so I took his blood while he's sat in the car, and then, took the blood sample into the hospital, and then I took him home, and as he's getting out of the car he collapsed but I remember thinking, I'd got a new car at the time, and I remember thinking, don't scratch my car.'

Kitty takes Adam through a whistle-stop of the events leading up to his arrival in A&E.

KITTY: Back home. Back into bed.

ADAM: So tired. So weak.

KITTY: And nobody knew why.

AUDIO – Adam's mum – 'I came home, and this sounds stupid, I thought, Adam, couldn't you even wheel the wheelie bins up?'

KITTY: Couldn't do one little thing for your mum.

ADAM: She didn't know what was wrong.

KITTY: Useless.

ADAM: She felt awful when she knew. She told me.

KITTY: And in so much pain. Hyper – sens – it – tivity.

            What did you do on Sunday?

ADAM: Went to the bathroom to try and have a shower.

KITTY: You collapsed! Phone the ambulance. Ne Na Ne Na. A and E.

ADAM: They gave me oxygen in the ambulance and the pain went away.

Hospital sounds.

Kitty and Adam are looking down at Adam in A and E.

ADAM: How do you feel?

KITTY: Where's the pain?

ADAM: Who's the Prime Minister?

KITTY: What day is it? What year is it? What's your name?

ADAM: Breath to this. As hard as you can. Push with your legs.

KITTY: Push with your arms.

ADAM: Has anything like this happened before?

KITTY: Has he been doing anything unusual, out of the norm, lately?

ADAM: We need to run further tests.

KITTY: They haven't got a clue, have they?

ADAM: They will find out what it is. Look at Emma, see.

KITTY: Your sister's on the phone.

ADAM: She's ringing Andy.

KITTY: Don't tell me, Andy's a doctor.

ADAM: And Andy's going to fetch a mate of his.

KITTY: A mate...?

ADAM: Who happens to be a consultant – in Neuropathy. Do you know what it is?

Kitty takes the role of the consultant.

KITTY: Not yet, but we will.

Kitty starts to examine Adam.

ADAM: I don't remember his name but I do remember he had a black beard and an East European accent. No, really, he did.

KITTY: You're going to need a lumbar puncture.

ADAM: Is that something I should be worried about?

KITTY: Not unless you're one of those people who've got a thing about having a six inch needle stuck into your spine.

ADAM: He was the first one who talked to me like a person. He made me laugh.

KITTY: So, the lumbar puncture, what was that like?

She curls him into the fetal position and holds the needle ready.

KITTY: Pretend I'm the four nurses who had to hold you down.

ADAM: It hurt.

KITTY: It hurt? Is that all you've got to say?

ADAM: It hurt.

Adam stands. Hospital sounds fade.

KITTY: What are we doing now?

ADAM: Waiting.

KITTY: Lying there, all wired up, you could be on Casualty.

Pause.

KITTY: House would be better than Casualty. Because even if you die on House at least you've got the satisfaction of knowing he's worked out what was wrong with you.

Pause.

KITTY: Look, I'm sorry but it's out of my hands. A person gets sick, I come in, try to help, attack the illness...

Pause.

KITTY: Problem is once I've started I don't seem able to stop.

Pause.

KITTY: It's just the way it is. Not really my fault at all.

Pause.

The phone rings – Adam and Kitty alert.

AUDIO – Adam's Mum – 'They rang us at two o'clock in the morning to tell us ...'

AUDIO – DR WINER – 'It's GBS....'

Kitty stops Adam who's about to speak

KITTY: *(To Adam – whispers.)* That's me – Gary – Barry Syndrome.

(To DR WINER assuming role of concerned parent.) What's GBS?

Adam stands apart – listening.

DR WINER: *'GBS is a rare inflammatory disorder that affects the peripheral nerves, the nerves that go from the spinal cord to the muscles and also to the brain stem.'*

KITTY: How does that stop him breathing?

DR WINER: *'If those nerves that go to the respiratory muscles that take the air in are damaged, then those muscles don't work and therefore you don't take a deep breath, you take any breath, you don't take enough air into the lungs.'*

ADAM: I don't understand.

KITTY: Excuse me a moment. Your nerves have a myelin sheath around them. Gary Barry...

ADAM: Stop calling it that.

KITTY: GBS attacks the myelin sheath and as it disintegrates it stops the messages from the brain getting to where they should, if you have MS...

ADAM: I haven't got MS.

KITTY: ...the sheath is permanently damaged, with Ga.. GBS the sheath repairs itself. Probably.

ADAM: What?

KITTY: Shush. Sorry about that, doctor, can you tell us what's the next step?

DR WINER: *So I think the most important thing is that everything is done to help the breathing, and to stop the muscles getting stiff, and to make sure he doesn't get any complications which usually means giving something to thin the blood to stop blood clots, and then give this course of immunoglobulin, then wait until the nerves repair themselves.'*

ADAM: I can't believe you've done all this to me.

KITTY: Excuse me, I need a moment. You got the virus. I was only trying to help your immune system get rid of it...

ADAM: Then stop helping.

KITTY: Yes, well, would if I could... Sorry about that, Dr Winer, back with you now. Can I ask is he going to get better?

DR WINER: *'The natural history of GBS is for it to gradually get better over a period of time, but over that time there has to be some support for the breathing, if the breathing is affected.'*

ADAM: Ask him what he means by 'a period of time'?

KITTY: What do you mean by 'a period of time'?

DR WINER: *'Normally you don't make a full recovery from GBS for at least a few months, and of course although about 70% or so, three quarters of people make a very good recovery, not everyone does.'*

KITTY: Does that mean he might not get better?

DR WINER: *'It does mean he might not get better.'*

KITTY: When you say he might not get better, do you mean he's going to die?

DR WINER: *'Only a very small number of people with GBS die, but I couldn't say it was completely impossible.'*

PRE TRACHIE.

Sounds start.

ADAM: Figures round my bed. Move... like a time lapse... my mum... Emma... Ryan... change places... but I never see them move. Move... Got to be able to move... Shift. Tilt my body... Legs have gone... It's like the tide coming in, climbing up my legs.

KITTY: Very poetic. Oh, your eyes are dry. Give them a blink.

ADAM: I can't, can I? I want to speak. Can I speak? No. My face has dropped. On the left side.

KITTY: Has it?

ADAM: Have I had a stroke?

KITTY: Have you?

ADAM: The right side's gone now. Perhaps it's a really bad stroke, if both sides have gone?

KITTY: But they told you...

ADAM: Get worse. Lose movement. Get better. Plateau out. Get properly better slowly. Oh... it hurts.

KITTY: Shame you can't tell them that. Listen, they're talking about you. Mumble mumble... run it's course... Mumble mumble... plateau out... Mumble Mumble Mumble... Pneumonia.

ADAM: Pneumonia!

KITTY: Pneumonia.

ADAM: Nobody's said anything about pneumonia. Have I got pneumonia? Why aren't you talking to me? Tell me, not them, I'm still here. Speak to me, talk to me, have I got pneumonia?

KITTY: His BP and his pulse is rising. We need to do his breathing for him. They're getting you ready for theatre.

ADAM: Shut up.

KITTY: They're going to give you a tracheostomy.

ADAM: I want to listen to the doctor.

KITTY: They're going to fit a catheter.

ADAM: Not a fucking catheter!

KITTY: You'll be asleep for two or three days and you won't feel any pain.

Remind you of anything? Sympathetic faces round the bed... looking down at the patient...? You must remember. Wasn't that long ago. Yours was one of the faces.

ADAM: My uncle...

KITTY: Bingo.

ADAM: He was dying. I'm not dying!

KITTY: I'm sorry I went on at you about the wheelie bins, said the mother

KITTY: Just relax. They know exactly what they're doing, said the sister.

KITTY: We'll all be here when you wake up, said the cousin.

ADAM: Ryan...? No. Not you.

KITTY: You're going to be fine, mate, okay?

ADAM: You're my brother. Say the kind of stuff you should say... say... you're putting it on... say, take no notice, he'll do anything for a bit of attention... come on... Why aren't you taking the piss out of me?

KITTY: You'll be fine, mate, I promise.

ADAM: I don't believe you. I don't believe a word you're saying. I can see your faces. Puffy faces. I'm going to die. You're lying to me, you bastards, you lied all the time!

KITTY: They can't hear you remember.

Sounds of breathing done by a ventilator, operating theatre ambiance.

Movement sequence to the audio.

AUDIO – Emma – 'We were all stood outside, it was, at that point it was a relief he was having that done

KITTY: We're going to operate. We'll keep you under for a few days, give your body a chance to rest.

(CUT TO)   *I could see he was getting really poorly, his pulse rate was going up, his blood pressure was going up, and you could see his body organs were really struggling to cope with whatever was going on.*

KITTY: You're going to be fine, we'll look after you, give you a rest from the pain.

(CUT TO)   *At the level his blood pressure was going up to there was no way he was going to survive it, he was going to have a massive heart attack or a massive stroke'.*

KITTY: On to the trolley, rushing down the corridor, lights flashing past over your head.

AUDIO – Katie – 'He went straight from the operation to ICU. It's not nice. It stops you, I think, a little, in your tracks, and you think, hang on, what's going on? I'm really quite worried. Why are the doctors not saying something? His body's stopped. It's frightening.'

Kitty holds Adam almost in a pieta.

AUDIO – Adam's mum – 'As he went in, I looked over and I could see a patient, like, sat, like, propped up in this, like over this bed or something, I can remember looking at her, and I said, at least Adam's not like that and she'd got Guillain-Barré, but I didn't know that, and I'm saying at least she's not like that, thinking thank God he's not like that, he's in here, but he's not like that but within a week he was.'

Kitty helps Adam to his feet and together they establish the space where his bed is.

ADAM: Where am I?

KITTY: ICU.

ADAM: I can't move.

KITTY: No.

ADAM: How many nurses are there on the ward?

KITTY: One.

ADAM: I can see two. The ceiling tiles. They're dancing.

KITTY: That'll be the drugs.

ADAM: What happens to me now?

AUDIO – Katie 2 – 'You kind of steady off, and then you drop, you drop to a really low low point very quickly and it takes a hell of a longtime to come back up, and I remember thinking, gosh, this isn't even the worst bit, it's going to get even worse.'

ADAM: What do I do now?

KITTY: Let's see. What would you like to do? Go for a walk, go for a run? What do you think you do? You lie there.

AUDIO – Katie 3 – 'What's to say everything comes back, what's to say it all starts working again, if it all stops, and he's on a machine, what's to say he not going to be on a machine forever. And if it goes further then that's... game over.'

ADAM: I'm not going to die.

KITTY: Of course you're not.

ADAM: I'm not going to give up.

KITTY: I wouldn't expect you to.

ADAM: I'm going to get better. I'm going to do everything.

KITTY: Of course you are.

Kitty steps away, watching him.

AUDIO – John Winer – 'The severity of the GBS depends on how badly damaged the nerves are at the time.'

ADAM: What does that mean?

AUDIO – John Winer – 'If the electrical tests show damage to the axons then that means the nerves are severely damaged and it's going to take longer to get worse.'

ADAM: I know, I have to get worse before I can get better.

AUDIO – John Winer – 'And if the severity of the weakness is very bad then that also suggests it's going to take longer to get worse.'

Movement through this section. Kitty moving almost inert. Adam speaks to the audience.

ADAM: You don't notice time passing the way you do when you're living your normal life, when you're not pumped full of every drug they can think of. There's a new rhythm to the day. It's like I'm sleeping, but I'm not asleep. It's not sleep. It's... slow blinking.

KITTY: Blink.

ADAM: They take my blood pressure.

KITTY: Blink.

ADAM: They take my pulse.

KITTY: Blink.

ADAM: They wipe my arse.

KITTY: Blink.

ADAM: Change my catheter. Blink.

ADAM: Roll you over to stop the bed sores.

KITTY: And, blink, you've got another visitor.

ADAM: I love getting visitors, but I'm so bloody knackered.

Kitty goes to the audience and finds a visitor.

KITTY: It's not one of your family. That means you're going to have to make an effort. First visit. You can always tell. The way they look at you. What do you call it?

Kitty asks the audience member to smile.

ADAM: The pity smile.

KITTY: They're going to ask you how you're feeling.

ADAM: As long as they don't touch me, it hurts when they touch me.

VISITOR: How do you feel?

Adam replies in a voice we can hardly understand and Kitty translates.

KITTY: Not too bad. They're going to want to know if there's anything they can bring.

ADAM: Of course there isn't anything they can fucking bring. I can't move, I can't eat, I can't read.

KITTY: Tetchy.

ADAM: What could they possibly bring me that's going to be the slightest use?

Kitty asks the audience member to ask if there's anything Adam wants.

VISITOR: Is there anything I can bring you?

Adam smiles and shakes his head.

ADAM: (*Adam speaks but although we only hear sounds but it's obvious that Adam is repeating 'Of course there isn't anything they can fucking bring.' Kitty translates.*)

KITTY: No, thank you very much.

Pause.

KITTY: Look at her/him now. See how s/he's trying so hard not to let her face show what's s/he's thinking.

ADAM: What is s/he thinking?

KITTY: That you look worse than s/he thought. *(to the audience member who she takes right up to Adam)* We don't want to tire him out, do we? Time to say goodbye.

VISITOR: Goodbye.

Kitty takes the Visitor's hand and makes as if to touch Adam who makes a horrified noise. Kitty thanks the audience member and takes them back to their seat. Adam gets up and looks down at himself.

ADAM: How do I look? I can't see myself. Tell me.

KITTY: Well, for a start you look really ill. Your hairs' long. It's dirty, greasy, and unwashed. You haven't shaved in an age. Your teeth need a good brush, your gums are falling apart, and your breath smells.

ADAM: That's not me.

KITTY: Yes it is. Your aunt took a picture of you when you were asleep. It's on her phone, do you want to see?

ADAM: No. Delete it. Now. And tell her, and anyone else, don't take any more.

He walks towards Kitty.

ADAM: Everything is your fault. You've done this to me.

KITTY: I told you, not my fault.

ADAM: The pain. You. The fear in my head that I can't let anyone see. You. The fucking indignity of it all. You. It's all you.

Movement with Adam trying to restrict Kitty, Kitty trying to escape. Adam is trying to make her look at where he was lying in the bed.

ADAM: Canula in the back of my hand. Trachie tube down my throat. PRN. Pulse and BP every hour. Look at me.

KITTY: No

ADAM: Look at me.

KITTY: No.

ADAM: Feeding tube down into my stomach. Aortic valve. A nappy and someone to wipe my arse when I shit myself. Look at me!

KITTY: No!

ADAM: Look at me!

He holds her upside down and forces her to look.

KITTY: I was only trying to help.

They both retreat back upstage.

KITTY: What if...?

ADAM: I won't listen.

KITTY: What if...?

ADAM: No... You put these voices in my head. No.

KITTY: This is it.

With Kitty in control, Adam gives in to his fears for the future.

ADAM: What if...?

KITTY: You're in a bed for the rest of your life? What if?

ADAM: I don't get my life back?

KITTY: What if...

ADAM: It's better to be dead.

Long pause.

ADAM: I'm going to get better. I'm going to run, dance, play football, I'm going to do everything. I'm going to get better. I'm going to run, dance, play football, I'm going to do everything. I'm going to get better. I'm going to run, dance, play football, I'm going to do everything...

As Adam's voice gets quieter Kitty is starting to move his upper body as if she was his physio leading us into the next period of his recovery.

AUDIO – Katie – transition out of ICU – 'He started getting better slowly, one of the biggest things was when he started to communicate properly...'

KITTY: Proper words instead of all that looking and blinking?

ADAM: Yes.

KITTY: Well done.

Movement sequence. Adam is helpless, Kitty is moving him through the exercises, her live voice heard alongside the audio.

Audio – Kitty – 'Push with your arms. Push with your legs. Harder please. Roll over and stretch.'

KITTY: Push with your arms. Push with your legs. Harder please. Roll over, and stretch. Extend your legs. If you don't cooperate – lift your arms – and do your exercises properly – lift your shoulders off the bed – otherwise you'll never get better.

ADAM: I can't do it...

KITTY: Yes, you can.

ADAM: I can't.

KITTY: Can. Can Can.

Kitty lets Adam drop on to a chair.

ADAM: Keep trying. You can do it. Stay positive. Look how much you've achieved so far. It's no good you telling me how much progress I've made, how brave I'm being, you don't know what it's like. When you've all gone, when I've stopped 'being brave' for you, you've no idea what keeps going round my head. I know one thing though. If I don't get any better at least I've got enough movement to... do what? Take some pills? Turn on the gas?

Pause.

KITTY: Stop feeling sorry for yourself, you can cope with anything, said the cousin. I know it's slow progress but you did more this week than you did last, said the mother.

Think about it, you're using your body for the first time in months, so just get on with it, said the sister.

ADAM: Don't you get it? It hurts all the time. Ridiculous amounts of pain. I am fucking trying but I can't ever do what they want me to.

Pause.

Bastards.
I always fail. Useless bloody body.

He clenches both fists. Stops. Looks at them. Unclenches them slowly and spreads his fingers. He repeats the exercise.

If I can't do their exercises, I can do mine. Yes. I bloody will. All day. Everyday. For as long as it takes.

He stops exercising his hands and starts on his face.

KITTY: What are you doing?

ADAM: Learning how to frown

KITTY: What are you doing now?

ADAM: Learning how to smile.

KITTY: And now?

ADAM: Why d'you want to know?

KITTY: Curious.

ADAM: Worried?

KITTY: Interested.

ADAM: Feel you might be getting beat?

KITTY: Tell me.

ADAM: Watch.

Adam tries moving his eyebrows.

KITTY: Nothing's happening.

ADAM: It will. Watch.

He does the Jim Carey eyebrows.

ADAM: There. I can do it. Jim Carey eyebrows, mate.

KITTY: Very good.

ADAM: Very good? It's fucking brilliant. I taught myself to do this when I was a kid. I couldn't do it when I tried before, now I can. How can you lose if you can do Jim Carey eyebrows?

KITTY: Impressive, you can move your eyebrows.

ADAM: Got something else for you.

KITTY: You can waggle your ears?

ADAM: My shoulders can dance.

Movement sequence – Shoulder Dancing. At the end of the sequence Kitty stops before Adam, watches him. Adam stops.

KITTY: Time to stick the vacuum down your throat. Suck the phlegm out of your lungs.

ADAM: Not this time. No need. I can cough it up.

KITTY: You haven't got the strength.

Adam coughs. He coughs up the feeding tube. Kitty sees and moves in with chair.

KITTY: Very good. You've coughed up your feeding tube. We're going to have to put that back in.

ADAM: No.

KITTY: Remember the first time. The plastic tube with the metal tip pushing at the back of

	your throat until you couldn't stop yourself gagging…
ADAM:	No, you're not. If I can cough, I can swallow.
KITTY:	Slowly working its way down…
ADAM:	Don't put it back in, please. Let me try eating. Something easy. Yogurt. I know you've got yogurt.
KITTY:	One drop in your lungs…
ADAM:	… and you can do what you like … please.

Kitty gets the yogurt.

KITTY:	Here it is… The Shittiest… Mankiest… Vilest… Most Horrible… Sickly… Institutionalized… Cheapest… Toxic…
ADAM:	YOGURT! Cool. Wet. Smooth. Strawberries! MORE! A taste. The first for weeks. Strawberries. My tongue is moving, slipping, sliding, moving in my dry cracked mouth. Yogurt…

KITTY: And none of it went down into your lungs!

ADAM: More... More!

Kitty eats the yogurt.

ADAM: Finish it. Have the lot. I don't care, there's loads more. I'm eating now. Properly. I'm getting stronger.

We start to see his strength returning.

KITTY: Are you?

ADAM: You know I am. When I'm strong enough they're going to move me.

KITTY: Where?

ADAM: To Chatsworth. The rehab unit.

KITTY: You think that'll going to be better than the ward?

ADAM: Loads better. I get speech therapy. Physiotherapy I can actually do. My food doesn't fall out of my mouth when I eat. I've got a wheelchair. I'm allowed out down the pub.

KITTY: But…?

ADAM: *(to the audience)* Chatsworth is mainly a respite ward for people with MS. There was this old lady and she knew she was getting worse, but when she saw me doing my exercises, getting stronger every day, she was happy for me.

There was a girl too, my age, she wasn't going to ever get well, but she championed me getting better. That killed me…
One day I ask them to wheel me outside. I'm alone. On the small lawn in the centre of the courtyard outside the dayroom – not wearing pajamas, not wearing one of those stupid gowns that does up the back and shows your arse, on this hot, early summer day I'm wearing my football shorts.

From the moment I collapsed in the bathroom my body has felt… limp. And limp's not a word you want to use about yourself when you're a healthy young man in your twenties. I'm not sure I want to say it out loud… but at this moment, lying here, the grass cool beneath me, clouds moving, the sun warm on my face, fresh air in my lungs… life is… returning.

Adam, still weak, goes through his exercises. Still limited but they've expanded from only involving his hands and fingers. Kitty comes and sits beside him.

ADAM: I'm going to run. Play football. Walk round a lake. Write, draw, paint…

KITTY: Feeling better?

ADAM: Dance. Take a dog for a walk. Climb a mountain — I've never climbed a mountain, I will climb a mountain.

KITTY: Still got a long way to go.

ADAM: Have sex. Wipe my own arse…

KITTY: Yes, alright, I'm very pleased for you. What's that smell?

Adam stops the exercises.

ADAM: Suntan lotion.

KITTY: You asked a nurse to put suntan lotion on you? You let her touch you?

ADAM: Yes.

KITTY: And it didn't hurt?

ADAM: Not enough for me to tell her to stop. I'm getting better.

KITTY: Can you get up on your own?

ADAM: Not today. But I will. I'm getting better. You're history.

Kitty leaves him on his own and sets up the 'bars' Adam gets up and sits on a chair.

KITTY: Small steps towards recovery. In the ward are a set of parallel bars at waist height. By the bars are two physios to help and encourage...

ADAM: Bully.

KITTY: Enthusiastically encourage. A mother to watch and feel every moment as if she was the one struggling between the bars.

Kitty indicates 'mother' in audience.

ADAM: And Adam. In his wheelchair. As ready as he'll ever be. I've got an impingement.

KITTY: The nervous system is like a piece of string, flexing and unflexing your muscles, and when the string is loose, everything works without you even having to think about it. When you go through a period of not being able to move hardly at all, as you have, the string gets tight, won't stretch, and that...

ADAM: ... is called an impingement...

KITTY: ... and is the cause of your pain.

Adam picks up the little wooden man.

ADAM: My body is like one of those little toy men made out of bits of wood held together with, kind of, elastic string. You hold it in your fingers, like this, and when you press the bottom with your thumb the body collapses. Work your thumb up and down and you can make him dance.

KITTY: Again. Again. Always, again, never well done, Adam. And every time he does it 'again' he gets more and more tired and his attempts at 'again' feel more and more pathetic.

ADAM: This goes on forever. Every day. Unless I sleep through and miss a session. Jiggle forwards on the chair. Lift my legs onto the floor. Move the foot plates.

KITTY: Hands on the bars. And... pull yourself up.

Adam does so and he's in pain.

ADAM: Again and again and again. They move my legs. I walk on the spot. One two one two. Then, with them still moving my legs for me I'm ready to 'walk' down the bar. One two one two. Again and again. Over and bloody over.

KITTY: What he can't seem to grasp is that his body has lost its strength and forgotten how to walk. Relearning that skill takes a long time.

ADAM: And then they told me.

KITTY: We think it's time you walked the bar on your own.

ADAM: Now?
Okay.
Hands engaged.
Arms locked in.
And push.
Holding my breath.

Strain.
Grit my teeth.

A moment of contraction in my body.
Arms are shaking.
And I push, and they're straight, and I'm upright.
I don't want to describe it as walking – walking is when you don't think about it, it just happens, this isn't walking - but it is holding the weight of my body on my two legs. I'm floating. I know there's a floor. I know my legs are there. They're not doing as they should, but, look, mum, I've got to the end of the bars.

KITTY: He did five steps. He says he only did four, but his mum knows it was five. She watched every one of them.

Adam and Kitty move the bars. Kitty steps forward, speaking. Adam stands where he is.

HOME.

KITTY: The next big moment came when he made his first home visit to the bungalow his parents had moved into shortly before his illness began.

ADAM: 2nd June 2009. Spokey Dokeys on my wheelchair. Oh, yes.

KITTY: Fun was it?

ADAM: Spokey Dokeys on your wheelchair? Serious fun.

KITTY: Staff from the ward came with him to assess whether it was suitable for his needs. As his mother showed them round, she pointed out the rails and the ramps and the handles, thinking, 'Thank God we didn't get round to taking all the disabled aids out'. Next he was allowed home for a whole day, then a weekend. Soon he was able to leave the ward for short periods of time. He went to dance class.

ADAM: Dancing in a wheelchair when you're not used to it is bloody knackering, but I didn't care. I got to go down the pub.

KITTY: Accompanied.

ADAM: First time they took me out for a drink my catheter slipped and the tube got caught round the wheels. Can you imagine? That was serious. Funny now though.

She looks round at Adam who hasn't moved. She waits, then she continues.

KITTY: At last the day came to leave the hospital...

ADAM: What about getting septicemia. You can't miss out getting septicemia. God, that was awful, very dramatic though. High temperature. Nurse in a panic. Ambulance. Hallucinations. The whole bit.

KITTY: But you recovered?

ADAM: At one point I was convinced I was having a conversation with the Grinch. But it was some bloke who'd got jaundice. We should do that bit.

KITTY: But you got better?

ADAM: Yes.

KITTY: So – when the day came to leave the hospital...

ADAM: I didn't get better straight away. It was touch and go for a while.

KITTY: One, you got better, two, we can't put in everything.

ADAM: It was in the September I went home. Five months later.

KITTY: I know.

ADAM: Then don't make it sound like it all happened over a weekend.

KITTY: Five months later, in September, the day finally came to leave hospital...

AUDIO – The sounds of life outside, blurred, distant, music, voices we recognise but we can't pick out what they're saying.

When they arrive home, Adam sits.

KITTY: Home.

ADAM: Yeah.

KITTY: That's good, isn't it?

She looks around.

KITTY: Where's your mum?

ADAM: Work.

KATIE: Emma?

ADAM: Work.

KITTY: Katie?

ADAM: Work.

KITTY: Your brother? Ryan?

Adam doesn't reply.

> At work.
>
> On your own. Home alone.

Kitty takes on the roles of the speakers, his sister, his cousin.

AUDIO – Recorded fragments of Kitty's voice saying the same words form themselves into a loop as she speaks and continue through the movement.

When Adam stands and moves, she follows him, and it becomes a movement piece based around his frustration, his depression and loneliness, their encouragement that he tries to block.

EMMA: You've had one to one nursing care. You've been the centre of the universe. Everyone's looking after you. Now you're alone. On your own.

KATIE: You think it's coming back. There no chance of that, and you're getting a little bit paranoid.

EMMA: Think of all the drugs you've been taking. You've got to get those out of your system before you start to feel normal.

KATIE: You need a bit of straight talking when you start to get flimsy.

EMMA: You're depressed, but it's the drugs, it's not you. It'll pass.

The voices recede as Adam is back where he started. Kitty comes and stands by his side.

ADAM: You're still here. You're going to come back, aren't you? You're not ever going to go away.

KITTY: I can't.

ADAM: I can't go through all this again.

Pause.

KITTY: You're a different person now.

ADAM: No, I'm not, I'm still me.

KITTY: Still you, but different. Ask your family. Ask your friends.

ADAM: You have not changed me.

KITTY: But what if I have? What if it's for the better?

ADAM: Don't give me all that suffering makes you a better person bollocks. What this is all about, really about, is I know you're inside me, and any time you want, you can mess my body about all over again and there's nothing I can do to stop you.

Adam refuses to continue the conversation. Pause.

KITTY: You should get some sleep.

Pause.

Adam gets up. Kitty sits.

ADAM: I can't sleep, can I? I'm exhausted, but there's no point in even shutting my eyes. I only fall asleep when my body gives in because it can't take anymore. I don't know if it's the drugs they've put me on, to get me off the drugs they put me on, or the GBS.

I stay awake most of the night. I play World of Warcraft. Hours at a time. I'm obsessed. Time, hours and minutes going past, doesn't have any relevance, time is no longer a concept. I play until sleep comes and I... pass out... in the chair or on the bed. I wake up. Eat. Sometimes wash, mostly don't. Mostly go straight back online and play some more. Now, it sounds stupid. How could I have wasted so much time? But then...

It was me doing something I could be good at. It was... a chance to escape the shittiness of the world. I had an avatar. I went on missions. I run, I fight, I hide, I move. I join up with other gamers, talk to them, become part of a team. Do you know what got me really mad? When my fingers and my arms were so tired I couldn't play anymore. I loved it. When I played, I stopped being alone.

Kitty comes and stands behind him.

KITTY: Because everybody's forgotten you and no-one comes to call.

ADAM: Because as soon as you're out of hospital they think you must be better. But you're not, you can't go out without help, you're stuck inside...

She makes him sit.

KITTY: All those things you were going to do. 'I'm going to run. Play football. Walk round a lake. Write, draw, paint…'

ADAM: How can I do any of that in this state?

Pause.

ADAM: You don't think I ever will, do you?

Pause.

ADAM: I'll bloody show you.

KITTY: Show me what?

ADAM: I'm going back to work.

KITTY: Up those stairs? Not in a wheel chair, you aren't.

ADAM: I'll be on crutches soon, I'm working on it.

KITTY: I bet you couldn't get to the end of your street.

ADAM: I bet you I could do. I'll do it now.

KITTY: You can't do it now.

ADAM: Why?

KITTY: Your mum's coming back off work early to take you to Jobseekers.

ADAM: I bloody hate Jobseekers. Employment support. Disability money. I said, I don't want it, I don't need it. But then I thought why not? I could use the money. I got a new TV, new laptop, more DVDs...

                My mum was so worried about me becoming depressed she said...

KITTY: If you want you can have a dog for company.

ADAM: And she hates dogs.

Kitty hands Adam a clipboard and puts a plastic identity card round his neck.

ADAM: I never got the dog.

HUMAN RESOURCES.

KITTY: We're here to discuss Adam's return to work. From a human resources point of

|||view we're anxious that if that's what he wants...

ADAM: We should do everything we can to make it happen.

KITTY: However...

ADAM: He can't walk.

KITTY: He needs a wheelchair.

ADAM: He needs crutches.

KITTY: He needs sticks.

ADAM: There are the stairs to consider.

ADAM: Health and Safety. Ease of access.

KITTY: Forgive me, I have a question – Is it possible to run a theatre workshop from a wheelchair?

Adam hands Kitty the clipboard and takes off the identity card.

KITTY: We're considering a phased return.

ADAM: No.

KITTY: It might be the best way.

ADAM: It's a part time job. Two hours running a theatre workshop. I'm not having a phased return for a job that lasts two hours.

KITTY: There'll have to be a risk assessment. He'll need to have someone in the room with him.

ADAM: Alright. Okay. Someone in the room with me. I'm fine with that. But as soon as I can make it up those stairs I'm back.

KITTY: All credit to him, he made it. His first day off crutches was his first day back at the Palace Theatre. We watched him go up those stairs on his hands and knees. I thought should I try and stop him, then I saw his face and thought, perhaps better not.

ADAM: Almost as soon as I got back I had to go and to ask for ask for time off.

KITTY: A hospital visit?

ADAM: My brother's getting married. I'm going to Cyprus.

GOING TO CYPRUS.

Movement sequence. Kitty taking on the role of Katie.

AUDIO: airport atmosphere, announcements, etc.
Katie – 'Cyprus, that was the big thing. I think it was frightening for him because he was out of his comfort zone'.

ADAM: I've been out of my comfort zone for the last two years.

                  'He was worried he was going to get it back'.

ADAM: Well, wouldn't you be?

What if I lose my meds? What if it comes back?

KITTY: If it did come back, which it won't, you'd deal with it.

ADAM: What if I get ill and I'm stuck over there? What happens then?

Kitty takes on the role of Katie.

KITTY: What if you just shut up and get on the plane?

Atmosphere fades and changes to - Adam outside their room, on the balcony.

ADAM: I've been out every day. To the pool. On the beach. To clubs. Bars. I feel better for just being in the sun. Still get so bloody tired. Some of my brother's mates don't know what to think – what's up with him, one day he's on crutches, the next he's not?

Pause.

KITTY: Adam?

ADAM: I'm sharing a room. With Katie, her boyfriend, and her mate, and her boyfriend. I spent the last year complaining nobody came to see me, now I can't move.

KITTY: Adam!

ADAM: I get these moments when I want to be at home. In my room. Shut the door. And not be... so far away. I'm having a fantastic time, yeah?

I don't think I feel right.

KITTY: We're going out. You haven't started to get ready and it takes you at least an hour to do your bloody hair.

ADAM: You go.

KITTY: What's the matter?

ADAM: I don't fancy it.

KITTY: What's the matter, I said?

ADAM: I'm staying in.

KITTY: No, you're not.

ADAM: I think it's coming back.

KITTY: It's not coming back, they told you.

ADAM: What if it is, though?

KITTY: There's no chance of that happening. They told you. Emma told you. You believe Emma don't you?

ADAM: Yeah.

KITTY: You're still a little bit poorly, you're still getting better.

ADAM: I want to go home.

KITTY: You've not stopped since we got here. Every day, every night, you've drunk more, eaten more than you have in months. You've been out in the sun. Think about it. You've done too much, too quick.

ADAM: I don't feel well.

KITTY: You feel tired. You're getting a little bit panicky, a little bit paranoid. You don't have to go mad, but you're not staying in, you're coming out. Get yourself sorted or we'll be late.

Pause.

ADAM: Five minutes.

KITTY: More like fifty five. He needs a bit of straight talking sometimes when he gets a bit flimsy. It's exactly what he'd say to me if it were flipped around. And he was okay, he was fine.

ADAM: Fine – ish.

I came home and carried on getting better slowly. Some of time I felt I was getting

	nowhere even when I was. A lot of the time I behaved like a pig. Sorry, mum.
KITTY:	Afterwards you think how did I get through that? But you just do, said the mother.
ADAM:	My walking improved.
KITTY:	You'd go home at night and get really upset, but you do it, you carry on, said the sister, but when it's all over you think, that really was a bit stressful.
ADAM:	The drugs were starting to wear off and I was beginning to be less of a pain in the arse – I think?
KITTY:	At the end it's a good thing, we've all been through it and now here we are, said the cousin, we got there, all of us together. You were one of the lucky ones.
ADAM:	I was.
KITTY:	If things had been different?
ADAM:	I'd be dead.

KITTY: You know what I mean.

ADAM: I don't know.

KITTY: Yes, you do. What did Katie say? When you were scared it might come back? Whatever it is, you can deal with it.

ADAM: I suppose so. You have to.

KITTY: Like the old lady and the girl you met on Chatsworth ward.

ADAM: Yes. I have days when I'm hypersensitive. Sleeping pills to take every night because my legs twitch uncontrollably, and I get hot, and cold, and I still get very tired…

KITTY: But to look at you no one would think you'd ever been ill.

ADAM: Very true.

KITTY: You still haven't climbed that mountain.

ADAM: Yeah, okay, one day.

KITTY: You danced again.

ADAM: I did.

KITTY: You found yourself a football team to join. He shouldn't have really, he looked okay, but he wasn't strong enough. His mates on the team...

ADAM: ...and moving swiftly on...

KITTY: ...before they found out what he'd had, called him, Ten Minute Adam...

ADAM: Because that was about how long I could play before they had to sub me. Not a problem anymore.

KITTY: I'm glad to hear it.

Adam takes out the little man.

ADAM: When something like this happens, you think, from now on my whole life will be different. I'll see everything with fresh eyes, the trees, the sky, the clouds, I'll stop and listen to the birds singing.

KITTY: You'll never, ever forget how wonderful it is to be alive.

ADAM: But you can't live like that, being ecstatically happy, all the time...

KITTY: Because, one, it would drive everyone else round the bend...

ADAM: And, two, you've still got to pay the rent. Sometimes I'll get a phone call.

KITTY: Adam, we've got a patient come in with GBS, do you think you could...? That's great, thanks very much.

ADAM: If they can speak, I listen. Then I tell them what to expect. I'll tell them the truth, what it was like for me, being locked in, the pain, being helpless, the fear, the boredom, all stuff I wish someone had told me.

KITTY: When someone tells you the truth it's frightening...

ADAM: But, honestly, it's better to know, and anyway, they might think, if he got through it, so can I. I tell them, don't go all 'why me?' That gets you nowhere. You haven't been picked out specially to hold the shitty end of the stick. Stuff happens. I tell them, if you're lucky, and there's a really good chance you will be, if you never give up, however it turns out, you'll deal with it. 'Cos that's what we all have to do, isn't it?

He collapses the little man, and lets it spring back up again.

KITTY: Time for your Billy Elliott moment, I think.

Adam dances and invites Kitty to join him.

THE END.

"*How astonishing, when the lights of health go down, the undiscovered countries that are then discovered...*"

Virginia Woolf – 'on being ill'

Our Crowdfunders:

We thank you for your support in helping us share Adam's story and to help raise awareness of Guillain Barre Syndrome & GAIN Charity.

Keep supporting the arts!

Clare Lindsay; Tony Kenneck; Andy Dobb; Robin Sheppard; Phil Hamlyn-Williams; Caroline Morrice; Jean Yates; Hal & Beth Branson; Victoria Elizaga; Ann Pownall; Reece Armstrong; John Halliday; Caroline G; Stella McCabe; Jo Stendall; Dean Krause; Basil Long; Ben Spiller; Helena Leanord; Janet Marshall; Drew Baxter; Debbie McAndrew; David Savage; Eleanor Field; Laura Lindsay; Ann Marie Wragg; Jean & Mick Randle; Lisa Wedgewood; Susan Graham; Fifth Word Theatre; Joanne Leveridge; John Tatlow; David Chriscole; Chris Jeffery; Katie Pownall; Kath Birch; Linda Somerville; Vicky Pownall; Ava Hunt; Craig Innes; Mandy Nicol; Michael Woodhall; Annabel Turpin; Shona Powell; Ros Oman; Kayleigh Hunt; Sarah Fox; Simon Hollingworth; Julie Colley; Emma Pownall; Matt Cawry; Tom Briggs; Phoebe Wall-Palmer; Beccy Freeman; Toby Ealden; Edward Boott; Danny Pressman; Kevin Farmer; Jen Wren; Kay Kane; Marilyn Ricci; Ashley Bates; Michelle Booth; Nikki Disney; Jane Gallagher; Jordan Dungworth; Claire Gaynor; Sheila Ridge; Charlotte Kemp; Alison Willcox; Emma McDowell; Ben Welch; Ben Rothera; Michelle Slack; Roxanne Saucedo; Tina Carter; Rebecca Slack; Chris Kirkwood; Steve Monk; Trina Haldar;

Alex Chapman; Karl Williams; Louise Fretwell; Steven Pryce; Carly Brookes; Dawn Hills; Caroline Small; Kate Smart; Aaron Gent; Julie Fox; Hannah Stone; Jodi Northcote; Rachel Dunne; Lisa Hibberd; Shelley Thompson; Nina Turner; Adam McCready; Bethany Sheldon; Maxine Dillon; Aly Manifold.